Swimming with Whales

Yogesh Patel

Skylark Publications UK
10 Hillcross Avenue, Morden, Surrey SM4 4EA
www.skylarkpublications.co.uk

First Edition: Swimming with Whales

First published in Great Britain in 2017 by:
Skylark Publications UK
10 Hillcross Avenue
Morden
Surrey SM4 4EA
www.skylarkpublications.co.uk

This book is sold subject to the condition that it shall not, by way of trade or otherwise, be lent, re-sold, hired out, or otherwise circulated without the author's and publisher's prior consent in any form of binding or cover other than that in which it is published and without a similar condition including this condition being imposed on the subsequent purchaser.

Yogesh Patel has asserted his right under the Copyright, Designs and Patents Act 1988 to be identified as the author of this work.
©2017 Yogesh Patel

ISBN 978-0-9560840-5-7

British Library Cataloguing in Publication Data: A CIP record for this book can be obtained from the British Library. Onix codes available on request.

Designed and typeset by Skylark Publications UK.

Cover Painting by ©**Meena Chopra.**

Printed and bound in Great Britain and through various channels internationally to be printed locally and distributed

All profits from this book will be channelled to the whale preservation and other literary charities.
Additional donations can be made through our website.

Word Masala and Skylark Publications UK are Non-Profit Social Enterprises ethically paying all taxes due in the UK.

Acknowledgements

Thanks for the cover painting
  © **Meena Chopra**

<u>Dedicated to</u>
  Lord Parekh | Lord Dholakia | Baroness Prashar

<u>Special thanks for the blurb:</u>
- Prof Meena Alexander, Distinguished Professor of English, City University of New York
- Michael Schmidt OBE FRSL
  Editor: PN Review, MD: Carcanet Press Limited
- Daljit Nagra, poet
- Zata Banks, PoetryFilm

<u>Thanks also for your support:</u>
  All Word Masala Award-Winning poets who are a great inspiration

<u>Thanks for edits and suggestions:</u>
  Brian G D'Arcy | Dr Debjani Chatterjee MBE | Reginald Massey

As a co-editor of Skylark, **Yogesh Patel** has published international contemporary poetry since the seventies. Currently, he runs Skylark Publications UK and the **Word Masala** project to promote writers and poets of the South Asian diaspora. He also edits *eSkylark*. Additionally, Yogesh is a founder of the *literary charity*, Gujarati Literary Academy, and has served as its president. He was a Fellow of the International Poetry Society and a Fellow of the Royal Society of Arts. He was awarded ***the Freedom of the City of London*** and, as a trilingual poet, has four LP records, two films, radio programmes, children's book, fiction and non-fiction books, including poetry collections to his credit.

Apart from being a recipient of the IWWP award, the International Scottish Diploma for the excellence in poetry, and a Hon. Diploma from the Italian University of Arts, he has won the Co-Op Award for the poetry on the environment.

By profession, Yogesh is a qualified optometrist and an accountant.

A short list of his work and achievements is listed at www.patelyogesh.co.uk

(Yogesh has been published by Under the Radar, IOTA, Envoi, Understanding, Fire, Orbis, IPSE, BBC, Muse India, Confluence, Asian Voice, Skylark, and others. He is also anthologised in MacMillan, Redbeck and other anthologies. He has read at many prestigious venues, including the House of Lords and the National Poetry Library, Southbank Centre.)

Index

At Sea

Yoga in the Kelp Forest	8
The Best Bet	11
Origami Whales	12
A Sea of Poppies	13
A Willow Whale	14
A Full Stop	16
Deflation	17
An Exclamation	18
A Giant Gob of Earwax	20
There They Blow	21
Extinction	23
A Very Rude Whale	25
A High Price	27
Whale's Sunburn	29
The Territory	30
Why Do I Care?	31
What Do I Do with My Large Brain?	32
One Ocean	34
Ink	35
Chariots of Fire	36
Wilma, the Teenager	37
Being Somebody	38

On Land

The Migrant Mangoes	40
A Strange Sighting	41
A Problem with History	43
Disenfranchised	45
Just another Whale	47
At Home with Homelessness	48
Whales Breaching in My Lounge	49

London	50
The Thames-Whale Skeleton	51
Namaste	52
SeaWorld	53
Neither Here nor There	54
Life after Death	55
At the Natural History Museum	56
A Whale and I	57
A Big Welcome	58
Gardening	59
Oh, Rama! Why, oh Why, Obama?	60
Not Some Gujarati	61

Skyward

A Strange Migration	63
Whale and Buddha	64
Apathy	66
A Whale Sermon to Man	67
Whale's Sermon to God	69
A Leap of Faith	70
God's Tear	71
A Spirograph Whale	73
Blowing Bubbles	74
Translucent Whales	75

'A word spoken on land
Is worth nothing at sea-'

Sujata Bhatt (from Poppies in Translation)

At Sea

Yoga in the Kelp Forest

Join the waltz in my space
Where the roused kelp forest
Slips free from time's grip
Currents wash ritually
Sun's holy myriad feet
Where is the bride in yoga?

The brushed grey interlocks
Artist's sombre green strokes
Touching the oxidised
Yellow, marking the past

These plumage-metronomes
Birds not claimed: All dead
Are not wretched ferns
In coitus entwining
Playing music on trillion
Sensual strings stroking
Silky sea surface
The majestic feathers
Fondling liquid lovers

Come, come, swim with me
Swim the lithe language

Like sea lions and seals
Roll free in silver waves
Learn to float like otters
From your office tables
Belly-up and no care
In the world, tranquil
Papers pushed aside
The boss can go to hell!
Such is the racket

Of holiday in yoga

Some say the kelp forest is
Sea witches' knotted ropes*
Don't come to get tangled
See, swim and learn the bliss

Distance yourself from
Brouhaha of gulls
Noisy herons and terns
Learn to swim like a whale
Creating a centre of
Uncharted cartography
A bubble of the inscape
Outside your lost dreams
This is the other you
Where you can draw pictures
With your boom and echoes
Cast over hundred miles
The radars of Facebook
And WhatsApp silenced
Use lengthy kelp ropes
Pull up a child in you

Come swim with us whales
To watch the undulating
Happy kelp forest
Kelp raining incessantly
Your world's conversed image!

The guns of your wars
Will be silent here and
The violence in trance
Like a shark flipped belly up!**

This is yoga, my friend

This is a fluid state
This is
बुद्धं शरणं गच्छामि।***
Buddham Sharnam Gachhami!
~~धर्मं शरणं गच्छामि। Dharmam Sharnam Gachhami~~
Kelpam Sharnam Gachhami!
~~संघं शरणं गच्छामि।Sangham Sharnami Gacchami~~
Samudram Sharnam Gachhami!

* *Sea witches and ropes: Many folklores feature witches selling to sailors magical ropes tied into knots to help them on a voyage. Pulling them in a certain way generated south-easterly or northerly winds.*
** *Shark trance: https://www.sharktrust.org/en/tonic_immobility*
****The Three Jewels Of Buddhism: Mahayana version http://tinyurl.com/kjle9yr
Instead of taking refuge in Dharma and Sangha, here the refuge is taken in kelp and the sea (samudra)*

The Best Bet

I can tear up the lone moon
I can pour cold water on the sun
But I choose to swim like a salmon
Wild, free, leaping, without a moan

Scheming Orcas will always be there,
Preying; catching you from nowhere

Sperm whales will stun you with a boom
There is always doom and gloom

Better not to be in someone's net
Wilderness is always the best bet

I can tear up the tides, the moon
I can dowse, eclipse the sun
But I elect to swim like a salmon
Wild, free, leaping, without a moan

Origami Whales

When you have no words
Sentences not streamed
Have a silent soliloquy
Street lamps' flickering tongues
Burning the midnights
With extracted whale oil
Have a fight picked with gods
Have the lone ocean empty
That won't take your tears

When the diner is Nighthawks

Don't drop a coin
In the jukebox
A black hole of
Intoxication
Keep it for the poet's hat

Return the drink to
The bartender
Fold the paper serviette
Create the origami whale

So, you too can
Breach the façade
And stare at the world
From poet's pages
Each a strange sighting

Yes, this is called
A whale lunging
Not a nose-dive

A Sea of Poppies

A beginner as I am
I question poppies incessantly
What is this mass destruction about?

Women and children
Are not the only casualties
War has no penchant
Have you absorbed
The blood of all men
To leave no names?

Sea Shepherd to the rescue at
The Faroe Islands!
But who will free
The Everlost* Whales
From a sea of poppies?

*Everlost: Please refer to http://tinyurl.com/gnotlt7

A Willow Whale

One shouldn't be alone in this world
And you know better
So you dive into green field
With your willow fin tail
Waving permanently goodbye

Not finding love you pop
Your head through the ground

Man is a magician
He cuts you in two halves
With the tail and the head apart
You none the wiser
Wondering what happened to the sea
So he fools you at Bristol city centre
With the fibre optics water

No one should be alone in this world
Even when one has been turned into a monument
So you still rejoice people
Coming to meet you, touch you
Even when you are a spiky dry willow

You never met my neighbour
- I don't know the name–
She died alone in her fish-tank
Dead for weeks
Hungry violent cats scratching windows
There are no monuments for her

No one should be alone in this world
So be gracious, my willow whale
You are dead as willow
But we come to visit you
Touch you
Even when you are a monument

A Full Stop

At every full stop
I have taken a deep breath
Dived to remain disappeared
As circles disappear, the centre too
You say the sea is disturbed
Give me a moment, then tell me where

A whale punctures the whirls
I do too

But to find a white lotus, *kamalashana*
I need to breach the depth
That harbours home
Creating a fresh full stop
Stirring encircling sentences

A whale migrates between two full stops
I do too

We are not about moons and stars
They don't point to our home
We swim in homelessness as home
A vast ocean of sharks

A whale doesn't know its home
I don't either

You call our coming, an unwelcome arrival
But my friends, we have never arrived
We are suspended in full stops
In migration's quantum sea

Deflation

A full stop asserts itself
Water flowering as waves

You blame the whale for the disturbance
You try to iron out creases in your tablecloth
The whole business of whale breaching
On your table is bizarre, you insist

The floating whale nation
Cannot boast nationalism
But it is a threat, you insist

So you punch the whale balloon
Hovering above us
Making the child in you cry

Why the whaling
When all is *very like a whale?**

**Very like a whale:* Taken from Hamlet, when he quickly changes descriptions of a cloud as a camel, a weasel, and a whale. Polonius agrees every time trying to accept each description as de facto!

An Exclamation

To break the liquid prison's tyranny
A whale, a tearing exclamation, breaches
The blue solitude's velvet
Flapping over the sky: Featherless
Mid-ocean. Nothing to add. Words
Forever stunned. Just drumbeats

The jetted bubbles of questions
Thousands. A fountain of words

To fall within; unanswered, perturbed
Diffused history, repeated
Myriads of white petals tossed
As offering to *Surya*
The whale dives as a question
To the yogic peace. The equilibrium
A faith ascertained. A whale effaced

Man's Sun scatters the bloody flowers
On the altar of Faroe's sea

God shivers rigged with bombs
Watching from the Sahara's waves
A faith ascertained. A man effaced

The exclamation sky-hops
To find its own heaven
Like suspended Trishanku
And Jonah's deliverance

*Surya means the sun or the Sun God.

**Trishanku, a character in Hindu mythology, has come to represent a status of being in a limbo. The sage Vishwamitra enabled Trishanku to ascend to the heavens, but the latter was refused entry by the gods and was left to drop to earth. Vishwamitra refused to accept defeat, so left him suspended in mid-air.

(A Poetry film of this poem is archived by the PoetryFilm Archive.)

A Giant Gob of Earwax

No fountain pens in the sea
A whale still writes a travelogue
In a six monthly gunge
In the vaults of its ears!

No trees in the sea
For papers or tree rings
Whale, the weatherman, writes
Own weather rings

A microscope decodes the language
Earwax of DDT and mercury, words
Man's nauseating pollution
Raging stress hormones
Cortisol for breeding
Testosterone for sexual maturity
The selfies of sex romps
Secrets written in a giant gob
Those waters swam
Distances chased

Travelogue in earwax
Not tantalising memoirs

A migration can be a sticky business
But it can stink too

I saw once someone change the seat on
The Londonistan Underground
For the curry stinks too
They called it racism
 Why? Asks a whale…

There They Blow

There they blow
Words as fountains
A chalk mountain
Blown to pieces
Night's blackboard
Stunned, speechless
Like my language
In Uganda
In February 1972

There they go
Click-cluck cluck
Tribal drumbeats
Mountain to mountain
A language thread
As an undercurrent
In the liquid air
The King of Scotland's joke
Such cultural claims!

Who are you, chameleon?
Why are you a whale?

There they are
The wild ones
The guitar plucks dancing
On the water currents
The liquid strings
Whose tunes are they playing?

They breached once
To say namaste
To welcome me home

There they blow
Now indifferent to an alien

Extinction

My happiness is a flower
It blooms in my heart
A sea within a sea
The white rose petals splashed-
Like flung-open wings
Where can the giant butterflies fly?
Where can the giant swans go?
Sadly, you are armed with
Nibs, numbers, white coats
And grey suits
Swimming the rivers of
Poker-faced corridors

A slaughter is not a research
The shores of Faroe are not poppy fields
No war hero has fallen
How come the man is still standing victorious?

When your child is dismembered
Wailing and crying, cut alive
The pain surrenders the mother to harpoon
A sailor sends a note home
'Sweet Caroline, we had a good day today!'

The temples tolling the bells
Words inscribed on the stone tablets
Are no different to a cling film
Holding a crab's terror
Taped and wrapped in
Tight, in total pain, panicking
Displayed on a Korean shop shelf

The winter is over
Not all birds will return home
Not all migration will reward a home

Why do the temples need bones?

Instead, if you can spare a tear
The sea will take it, hungrily
For the bones you took from the migration

A Very Rude Whale

Damn it, screw you for what I care
And the whale unleashed itself
Bolting into heaven's bottom
Punching through the ocean's plain
Facial expression, a shimmering fabric
Rejecting permanent suspension in
Ever clutching amniotic fluid
To be born free, to be the other

But the womb has gravity

What else can the whale do?
But to give the heavens the finger
Against lonely skies and forlorn emptiness
Then the might of gravity
Brings it down, plunging, splashing
There! It returns to the womb
As *Shiv ling* to a *yoni*
It penetrates the hymen
First tearing with violence
Then gliding into lustful
Current with a phallic force
Shaking off the lingering parasitic beliefs

This is the quest, the quandary, the jostle
A tug of the soul and the life
The one that's also the other
The one that pulls out from the other
The one that returns to the other

You know, the flesh may want to flee
But only as the sea

A whale can be clouds, rain
Lakes, streams, rivers and ice
Its soul still returns
To the deep blue sea
The sea is oblivious, the soul too
The one that's also the other

That's the might of womb's gravity
You can't leave

A High Price

All that unruly splashing
Poseidon's backside lashed
You have something to insist
To your persecutor
Without Him you have no ID
A bond with the tormentor
Hardly anyone listens to you
Yet making a point is
All that you can do
Like all those dissidents
Hunger strikers
Against tyrannies

So when you escape
You escape with
No care for your death
Taking refuge in the Thames

But no one told you
You can't *fly* nor
Can you *walk* with
Men touting guns
Who have imprisoned God
Who have imprisoned man

Your essence lies in
Swimming free in the depths
Within a creation untouched

So, why this desire to give up your liquid cage?
Why this breaching, lunging, spyhopping?
Why the lashing of a fluid furtive space?
Why not remain captured in freedom?

Asylum as the Thames whale
Has a price very high

Just ask some of us

Whale's Sunburn

All those sunburns
And no holiday snaps
Whales can only record them
As blisters and burns
Been there, done that
Be they blues bluer
Sperms browner
Fins greyer

No need to sleep under the UV lamp

There is always one
A pale Brit in Baja
In his Union Jack boxer shorts
Asking a sperm whale
As he does to any Indian,
'Enjoy this weather, don't you?
No need for sunscreen, eh?'

A whale blows her nose crudely
She can't be bothered
To comment on someone's skin
And swims away
To the sea of better sense

The Territory

The territory means circling the young
Protecting them from the killers
The territory means circling the food
Trapping trout and squids for a feast
The territory means getting planktons
To light up the runway
Planktons to the prey
The territory means a dive to the bottom
Ignoring the sunken treasures of armada
The territory means a song travelling
Hundreds of miles for love
The territory means not the grave
But to disperse as an ocean
The territory means the waters lapping
All borders, including the territorial rivers
The territory means my memory
Your regrets, your aggression
The territory means breaching from oneself
Beyond seas to grab a name
Wilma the only whale
Loved to the end
The territory means the end of my story.

Why Do I Care?

Why do I care?

You're my wilderness
You're the depth, strange
Expanse, forbidden
Yet space to play

Knowing me and
Taunting my ego
You light up my streets
With your brain, history
Bright flickering tongues
With silent words
You define clearly:
My space

Why do I care?

For you surface
From my soul daily
As at Baja
Allowing gentle strokes
By a child I lost

What Do I Do with My Large Brain?

I don't argue for one, I am a sperm

Love is a memory, but
When you are with it, it is ROM
In Alzheimer, it is RAM,
Between each switch off, you are lost
I eat too many fish, so no worries

My brain is better developed
Than leaving 'now' out
When your wife asks you
To put the rubbish out
She means now, at this moment,
'drop everything'
No one needs a brain
for such trivial matters

Ganesh writes with cartographic sense
In my 7.8 kg brain of 8000 cubic centimetres
What do you mean by words?
Do they make you better?

There is a difference between living on the land
And non-stop swimming in the tangible expanse
You have many years to think
Without doing anything
Why do I need to colonise Mars
When I can't leave my home?

When I feel thousands of miles and
Talk without a landline or a mobile phone
When I want every swim or a dive remembered
Where my loved ones were hunted
For hundred years
It is a lot to store

What is a library?

Without music
You have nothing
So I store my original songs
Connecting families and tribes
About how I feel
I make friends
With a duel in Qawwali miles apart
Whistled, exchanged and improvised
To love and reminisce
To say I loved once
To say I was loved once
To say this is home
To say this is who I am

But I am aware
This is not how you know me
I am a bloody foreigner
And to cling on to my identity
You want to re-write
I need my large brain
So scoot
Get lost

One Ocean

Tell the ocean
Not to be fooled by a man
Holding a broken mirror
Peddling a lie
That it shows an ocean divided

Whales will tell you
There is only one ocean
There are two points
A place to feed
A place to breed

The rest is the abracadabra
Of a migration

Politicians will never tell you
Why there is no one nation
Why they are holding a mirror

Ink

i have not stood
at the shore sliced from a sea
that is blood
dipping a fallen feather
of a ruffled seagull
to write a report on a genocide
as a poem

blood cannot be red carnations
food is a fine excuse
when you are not starving
ritual is the other
it's all in the purpose of a knife

whales swim with me
in a liquid close-knit village
in the inner quiet space
with civilisations silent
with words' drumbeats
played as a click-cluck Morse-code
offering a poem
you can never write

you write poems with
items in your ambience
cluttered in rhythms
postured in descriptions
dancing, shouting, in spoken words

your poems revel in
washing off the red ink
in the sea

Chariots of Fire

The wave had an upper hand
The sea was at its command
A race to the finish, a wager
Whale too won't cower
And so it began

The wave is all deception
Disappearing, not diving
Miles apart; rising, falling
Opening up its belly
Delirious, reckless
Like a gargantuan hand
A palm of a large tsunami
Trying to grab the whale
Toss it, throw it

The whale runs deeper
No fuss, just whistling
Nothing to prove to anyone
And when the wave is done
Like a lover fully discharged
Whale keeps racing to migration
For that's what matters

You can be a storm, hurricane
A vortex or anarchy

Only the one who swims deep
Knows the secrets of a true conquest

Wilma, the Teenager

Just like any teenager
You thumped the surface
You sprouted the noise
You whipped the waves
You click-clucked your say
You jumped to conclusions
You nose-dived to hurt
You flip-flopped your way
You ran amok uncontrollable
It wasn't about the drugs
It wasn't about the sex
Hell, it wasn't about anything
So, when nothing worked
To get your own way
You ran away from home

Just like any teenager
You decided you don't
Need anyone, you'll survive
You didn't want to listen

You didn't want to reason

Just like any teenager
You took the wrong alley

The rest is history

Being Somebody

In the end it only proves
You were noticed, named
Only when you left home

"If you don't become the ocean,
you'll be seasick every day."
— Leonard Cohen

On Land

The Migrant Mangoes

Those of us who fell off a mango tree
Somewhere near the Mombasa sea

Unwanted, not ripe, black, sour, trodden upon
Were unclaimed by nations as their own

Then we arrived as pongy rotten "aliens"
In Canute's lap, the tides engulfed us
Wilma the migrant whale, lost, probing
Came to look us up, the surplus
Died of the shock of all Hocus Pocus
Her and us always foreigners
Hell with these snubbed-upon mangoes
No doubt, God had some other plans
Ted Hughes' Crow laughed at a chaos!

Victimised as a helpless Hindu
Alien Mango! You *are* booed as Urdu

Nurtured by the rivers of blood
Why? O'why? You fell with no thud!

No one knows sweet Alphonso
On this intimidating shore
Boatloads come with bemused whales
They are not Indians anymore!

* *'Ted Hughes' Crow'* refers to Crow by Ted Hughes

A Strange Sighting

Born alien in the incubator in Kenya
The Indian packaged to India, in Karanja
Born a foreigner, the citizen of the UK
Finally, dropped in the 'bloody' Tiber as a 'Paki'
The Thames, all grey and cold
The sun in hiding in the rubber stamps
Canute's Royal Commands
Echoing in the marches and riots
It was a different excitement to
A whale arriving in the Thames

What can a lost whale do?
Swim, walk, or fly?
Now that it is in the shallow waters, an alien
Walling banks so close
Deafened by own echoes
What can an alien do?
The migration is complete
The last breaths on these banks

What a curious object!
A whale that has lived in London

A house away from home
A stranger in own home
A house that is still a passport
With no meaning to born British

I do watch often the reel
Whale escorted out of the Thames
Never returning home

Yogesh Patel
A strange sighting!

A Problem with History

You insist I have no tales
To spawn history
A drop of water, you say
Can't be pinned to a date
And to the time
Like your stained *Palace*
Tales to tell of
Kings' and queens' treacheries
Anchored in blood and feuds
The Great Fire, 1834
Big Bang and Guy Fawkes
I am not a historian
The sea is not a monument
Knowledge is a vast liquid expanse
A drop, irrelevant
I have no names to drop
Have no passport proving my roots
No volume of water mine
I am but a lost whale
You watch, you take photos
Return home holding your picnic basket
Safe in your sanctuary
Feeling none of my pain
Fears, tears, and homelessness

So tell me
Why is my skeleton hanging as history?
Why are my bone temples boasting history?
Why the harpooned mother's foetus extracted
Is preserved in a stone tablet?

Are you asking me to thank you
Because I don't need to light up your paths
With my brain oil anymore?

I am not a historian
The sea is not a monument
I remember the moments I lived

History is your guilt

I am just another whale
The swimming water
It formed a shape
It will merge and disappear
I can't be pinned to a date or time

Disenfranchised

A near miss
Not one of 'Midnight's Children'
An African, an Indian and the British citizen
The all-in-one child
Orphaned by the Nile
Forsaken by the Thames
Abandoned by the Ganges
Sings in a school assembly
Asserts he is loved by history

He salutes the flag
Muttering, 'And who are you exactly?'
Blyth's reed warbler and olive-backed pipit
With sky under their wings
Sit on a pole with thoughts of nests
Far across the sea

The child learns from them the sky
Paces like a 'Caged Bird'
Someone opens the cage
'Bloody British!'
The child jets off
Clutching his British passport
Only to be rediscovered
As an alien

Haunted still by the rhythm of
Idi Amin's army boots
Nehru's bogus promise
Hum Nehruchachake pyare
(We are the children Nehru Uncle loves)
He meets Wilma the Thames whale
Watches in desperation
Her rescue. Then bones.
Wondering in which museum he would
Leave the Nehruchacha child's bones

Defeated he wanders dazed
Muttering
We are apostrophes
We are the bones
We are the bones
We are the bones

Whale and I

**Midnight's Child*ren' refers to Salman Rushdie's book and 'Caged Bird' to Maya Angelou's poem

Just another Whale

Like many a man of history
You took a wrong turn
To find yourself becoming
Naturalised as the Thames Whale
In a far distant land
Of fear and discordant noise
Now as disparate as one of
Us: Chinese, Negro, Asian
A damned undertaking indeed
Drowned in the deafening holler
Of passports, immigration control, visas
Religious labyrinths, Nazi chants

You, of course, won't realise
This, until you're a skeleton
You never migrate from the state of migration

Stop swimming
Stop migrating
And you are dead

Not all whales can be the Thames Whale
Not all Patels can be Dev Patel

At Home with Homelessness

Well, you thought the death was so withered
You wanted to emancipate yourself of any guilt
You wanted to recompense your own relived death
You wanted to be sure that's how you went

When they escorted your circus
To your home, the ocean
In a cradle of misunderstandings holding you hard
Your abating breath challenging dimming hopes
They kept baptising you to the end
As if your soul will ascend to the light
As if you will redeem yourself eternally
You cried, and you worried and you prayed
You had found the love you can't have

Yes, you were loved, as never before
Yet, you were only an expat whale
Neither here nor there in the Thames
No passport, no visa, only a misfit
You could not be housed

Your homelessness tossed
Between two worlds
How do I house you?
I make you somebody
I care and show love
That's a home away from home

In death, you're at home between homes
Is this why you came
To tell me where my home is?

Whales Breaching in My Lounge

She came to the Thames
With the dark curious eyes
Suitcase of foreign fears
Thirst, hunger and prospects
Were *not* the reasons
Lost, misguided, she died
No visa, no passport

The only thing she wanted
Was to show you
She could *be* somebody
The oceans couldn't hide her

She migrated to be the Thames whale
To be somebody, to be remembered

No, she didn't come to preach religion

Now I see the Mara Crossing
Boatloads, brutal, stampede
Fight to the finish, cruel
All for a hated steppe as home
A religious invasion

The EU stood dumb as an ocean on the land

What do I do with
The whales that are not the Thames whales
Breaching my lounge?

London

1.

Edification

My brain oil has lit
Your dark London alleyways to guide
Are you enlightened?

2.

Like Cleopatra's Needle

Like the Needle let the whale spread its fin-wings
Take a dive into a bluestone sea frozen
Let the shower of splash douse the Mayor's den
A plaque for the whale he may then sign

The Thames-Whale Skeleton

I was the sea that became flesh
The creation to learn to fear men
As Gods have always known

Like you brainwash children
Like you steal their language
My dialect erased with radars

I am a skeleton sculpture
That has jumped out of my blubber
A puppet on a dance floor
A courtesan, a display to devour
Monumental sea as a glass cabinet

Can you ask Anish Kapoor
To enliven my innards
Blood-red rioting loud unhinged?

Namaste

If a flame was a whale
Saying *Namaste*
Rising from the sea
Of well-oiled words
A spill
Posturing as a shy lamp
Splitting the darkness like
The Yamuna with a new-born Krishna
Allowing you to cross
Then treat the light as ink
Dip the feathers you took
From your ruffled hawks
Write a poem painting hope
Vocal of all your tomorrows

Oil is yours
Words are yours
The spill is yours
The Yamuna is yours
Krishna is yours

The whale is not spyhopping
It is just saying
Namaste

In Hinduism, Yamuna and Krishna are entwined in the story of Krishna's birth. When the oracle ordered Krishna's father on earth to take the newborn Krishna to Gokul, the Yamuna allowed a passage by breaking up its flow in the middle.

SeaWorld

Born and bred in homelessness
A home that is a pond, a migrant's world
I have to perform: every move watched
Corrected with a man on the nose!
I am a damned foreigner
If released in the wild
It means a fresh alienation
Returning home as someone else

The formation dance here: slavery
The formation in the wild:
Means to hunt as a pack
Creating waves as a family
To topple the seal from its
Shaky small ice island
Is only a spiritual world
The hunt is a social bond
The hunt is a cultural home
The hunt is a language

Pleasing the spectators
Delighting the masters
To earn the scraps for a living
Is not the avant garde art
This pond is a beggar's delight
In this mini – *virtual* - sea
Are torn alien cultures, trapped
Freedom is a chasm, your version

A sea is a scary place
If your home is the SeaWorld
I am a migrant afraid of home
Homelessness is my sanctuary!

Neither Here nor There

Returning within these walls
Scratched violently with fingernails
A fear of lizards raining
From the white blood-sucked ceiling
Keeps me awake wildly
But this is not a womb
The foetus fears home elsewhere

I was born with a rejection
The ocean I cannot breach
The foetal position
 Doesn't deliver me back to
The safety of a womb

So, when I stand next to
The homeless roving whale
I wonder if we are stuck
In the endless birth canal!

No one can correct where I come from
No one can expunge my origins
No one can mould me into some alien
No one can understand that
A journey from home to home
Is not a migration

My skin is the Thames whale
In limbo and petrified
Entered shunned in an estuary
Stuck; neither here nor there

Life after Death

What is it that requires of us
To extend to the far-flung
Eternity, the universe
Abandon emotions
To insist us as souls?
What is beyond it, us?
What are we beyond bones?
If you were ever a rose
Seasons mattered to you
If you were ever a whale
The world was once a sea
The world was once a home

There is no sea or home
When you're a skeleton
There is no universe
Why must a season matter?
Why must the sea matter?
Your home that never was
Yours, why must it matter?

And yet, you hang thoughtful
Insisting your mute bones
Prolonging the anguish
Of all that you ever were

At the Natural History Museum

With all its might
The mother ocean
Can't claim you now
Won't claim you now
Except as a non-resident
Alien
The border patrol has declared
You've crossed the estuary
You are a damn foreigner, you are

Yes, you are
Nothing but the 'Thames Whale'
You came as an immigrant
You die as an immigrant
You are a bloody foreigner
And in between, they'll do their best
They'll keep you out of their river
They will search you and research you
They'll escort you out
They'll debate you
Hell, they'll cry over you too
You're an outsider, an intruder
You may not reach
The Tiber to make it bloody
But you are locked in
To beach at the Thames

I can't fathom -
Posturing in a glass cage, your new world
Stripped to bones -
Why are you still smiling
As a brainless skeleton?

A Whale and I

Let us bring the sunshine
Through the stained glass windows
Tinted mosaic, held by the lead renaissance
Christ, angels and the fallen
To define us

Let us bring the sunlight
Redefining the taciturn darkness
Through the veils of waves
A woven thin silk, undulating in irrelevance
Making the first 200 ft depth a hub of life
The language wanting no expression

For both have the same job
In a cathedral or in sea

If I can leave the dark *open* prisons
Without gods and devils
And you, from the clutching sea
Deeper than 1000 ft

We won't need to meet at the Thames as immigrants

We will be defiant
We will not be extinct
Extinguished

Will anyone notice
We would have sky-hopped
As *Namaste?*

A Big Welcome

There is nothing new
In feeling alienated
In your own cold home

Welcome to the Thames
Its heart isn't big enough
It's your new cold home

One day we will meet
We will compare notes

Gardening

Dear Wilma, the whale
If you ever thought
You'll hold shovels
Fork the soil and
Turn it to plant
New bulbs and wait
For Daffodils
To declare spring
You are more fool
Than I ever thought

I had no such
Dreams, still I'm here
Watching the man
Next door digging
The time that would
Betray him daily

Oh, Rama! Why, oh Why, Obama?

'Excuse me, can I ask you a question?'

With all glassy blink from a mantelpiece
Like a prankster's framed cheeky smile
Dunked, muddied in the Thames' history
Wilma the whale flicks a woman's tongue
'How come the stuffy dons
The absurd scholars
Gave the Nobel Prize to Obama
Before he even pooped anything?'

'Indeed, one's poop is *perhaps* everything
Researchers spend days in puzzles
Sifting through my poop
To discover my secrets
To define me from my poop!*

Yet my poop is not worth the Nobel

So yes, can I ask a question?
Why, oh why, Obama
Before he even pooped anything?'

The power of poop, the circle of life:
http://blog.education.nationalgeographic.com/2014/04/07/th
e-power-of-poop-the-circle-of-life/

Not Some Gujarati

I am a blue whale
Not some Gujarati

In this liquid void
I twist, coil, and breach
Not to make money

I craft a landmark
Ever evanescent

Don't teach me Monopoly
My wealth is waters

I am a blue whale
Not some Gujarati

'God is a good fellow, but His mother is against Him.'

Ted Hughes

Skyward

A Strange Migration

(Dedicated to Umashankar Joshi and Suresh Joshi, the two Goliaths of Gujarati literature)

To have been blessed by two
Opposite alien poles
Baja and Alaska

I eternally swim lonely shores
Between gravity and space
To make oceans feel small
Like blue whale's journeys
In a migration cage

How do I explain
Watching with the suspended eye sockets
From the Natural History Museum
I am stripped off my skin
I am stripped off my gut
And that
I am hanging from the ceiling of this nation
As a curious object
?

Whale and Buddha

When you emerge airborne
You have your weight
Swim in depths and you are lighter
Nothing to do with dharma or karma
It's just plain science

Buddha needed a tree to be the Buddha
Where can whale find such tree in a sea?

She has remora and the daemonic lamprey
Buddha has no baggage

Whale never met Buddha
For he would have preached
The answer to transcending is
Not, always, in breaching
Diving within is also freedom
Homecoming

They insist I know where my home is
They call me a 'Paki'
Born British in Kenya
But always an Indian
A non-resident Indian!
I'm supposed to be at home
A stranger in my home

It is said, clouds are just oceans flying
Over deserts, seas and continents
They too always return home
So I suppose, man is a home in man

You don't need Buddha, my dear whale,
Accept your oceans
When you emerge airborne
You have your weight
Swim in depths and you are lighter
Nothing to do with dharma or karma
It's just plain science

Do not come looking for answers in
The Thames
I have found none ..

Apathy

ॐ सूर्याय नमः
Sun, I thee bow

The blood that you stage
As you rise, to bury the sea
Belongs to man's commerce
A leviathan you made swim
Laments within the depths
Echoing the mountains sunk
Still deafened by the shells
Exploding her calf
Harpooned, sliced opened
Mother's wailing is not a whale song

No prayers for the Sun
Submerging into blood
That darkens into nightfall

Whale, resigns to life
न तत्र सूर्यो भाति
Where there is no Sun

And yet
Sun, I thee bow
ॐ सूर्याय नमः

A Whale Sermon to Man

When the sea that holds you
Feels like a burden
Breach. Bolt out to grab
The stars, the sky, the sun
Shed the weight
To feel the full might of
Your gravity
Your blubber's tenacity
Will take it to shake off
Barnacles you collected
All your life

The scornful sea *is*
Always a family
Let it take you back
Even with its titanic slap
The ties in life are enduring
-The sea, the constant swim-
Beach from them and
You're a carcass, bones
Good for a museum

Why must be every bone
A pagoda at Vung Tan?
Why must be every bone
Rejoiced as a festival
Adorned with garlands
Street performances and songs?

Alas, some are carcasses sunk
Hidden from the world
In the creeks of Faroe Islands
The truth is not always facts
It hides in the creeks
It will never serve you
You are its victim

Hence, when the sea that holds you
Feels like a burden
Breach. Feel the full might of
The gravity
The life

Whale's Sermon to God

The floor crumbled to dust
The heaven fell in horror
All sank to the bottom
To become the blue lonely darkness
The whale breached fully
To spray empty the sea
There they blow
To make a room
For the falling Gods
And eject the hell
To the upper world
Hell there
Heaven in the pits
Adam and Eve flung
To explore the land of illusions

Whale spyhops to protect
Gods from the words
Man has written down as His

God pathetic in the deep
All alone, like a soul
Blue, deep, and cold
Oh, His desperate desire to exist
Like all His creation!

Whale warns Him
'Go to man if you must, but
You serve as his slave.'

A Leap of Faith

Abandoned by the birthplace
Idi-Amin *Adelie* penguins
Putting the boot in
The *Emperor* penguin chick
Struggles, stops, wonders
Should I? Shouldn't I?
At the borders
At the edge of a cliff
At the frightening first plunge
Into heartless ocean
A new country!

The warmth of father's pouch is
The motherland lost
What can you do when barbarians ride in?

You summon a leap of faith
To convince you
No one owns your home but you
It is where you find it!

Jump, jump, you stupid
Someone always pushes you
It is a jump from the old home
There's a new beginning in every jump
Orcas always ready to pounce

Every Mara Crossing is a leap of faith

* *Barbarians* refer to C P Cavafy's poem *'Waiting for the Barbarians'*. (**Inspired by** *Snow Chick - A Penguin's Tale,* BBC One documentary
http://www.bbc.co.uk/programmes/b06t3sk9)

God's Tear

What a glory to watch whale's sculpture!
Ghostly splash-wings skywriting
Swan's white twinkling
Sky's face all white
Finally, the water-wings shed
All a passing glory
The life can be as pure as that
Not wanting any meaning!

A life then escapes with its flesh
To sea's uncharted crèche

The ephemeral water-wings
Exhausted. Dispersed
Two worlds, sky and sea
Blended as solitude
No gulls or herons or terns
To fill the water-soaked God's silence

It was the moment when
God cried
Why did He create the man?
Why did man institute religions
Installing gods that never existed?
His tears were the seas
He filled them with whales, the life
While the man coloured the land red

But no crèche could hide the whales
And men above God
came in their gunships
To hunt God's creature
To silence Him again

God's tears are hope
You cannot wipe
Man wants to be God
Forget a torment, God's tear
From which all creatures crawled

So how long will whale survive?
Until all is undone?

It is lovely sunset
What a glory to watch whale's sculpture!

For now
The sun will rise tomorrow

Suryam Sharnam Gacchami
Buddham Sharnam Gacchami

Rejoice the yoga in the kelp forest

Genesis 1:21-"And God created great whales and every living creature that moveth, which the waters brought forth abundantly, after their kind, and every winged fowl after his kind: and God saw that it was good." - King James Version (KJV)

A Spirograph Whale

In a Spirograph coitus
The word-Amiga-Lemmings
Sketch strands of meanings
To find us as exits

A spurn whale
Breaches in the virtual space
A sea between us

I dream butterfly-nettings
You weave poppies
Both in the oceanic wilderness

We sail in a paper boat

The tired whales
Collapse in the untangling lines
Liquid lines disperse in wave-ripples

Everything is now quiet

It is a mystery
How the origami whales
Spun into Spirograph whales
With my efforts to give them
Their sea left absurd

Blowing Bubbles

I can't croon Dean Martin[1] when
I let the bubbles ascend skywards
The popcorn moments are not
Bubble whips of liquid lyrics
To lure salmons and herrings
They are spiralled bubble nets
A hunt: Nothing romantic

The West Ham United[2] fans
Shouldn't expect me to score goals
With footballs of bubbles

Fear draws you tight to your own kind
Ask anyone in a ghetto
Huddled shoal, spiralled densely
The sea surface lobtailed
A bubble cloud to corral
I use your slave-merchant tactics
Then as you say
the 'bastards' are caught!
But that's you

What a feast it is of
The shoal in coned bubbles!
Make the inverted Christmas tree
Dressed in blown bubble baubles
And make it a business of an angle
At the overturned top
When you are at sea!

[1] Refers to Dean Martins' famous song, 'I'm forever blowing bubbles'
[2] *Blowing Bubbles* is a popular magazine for the West Ham United fans

Translucent Whales

Poachers chopped the sea
Into Lego bricks
Stacked up as a spreadsheet
Remove one cell
The formula still works
In such liquidity
Someone added whales
To hear their songs

With this last poem
Carefree whales dive
Unaware of man's
Calculations

Emerge in my peace
As six paths of
Samsara as
Ishana Yamada's
Translucent whales[1]

Let's swim finally
You in six paths
I in six senses

---

[1] *Ishana Yamada's six translucent whales:*
http://tinyurl.com/k45legv

Poet-publisher-activist Yogesh Patel's latest collection
Swimming with Whales
is an awesome *tour de force* that has as its recurring metaphor the largest animal on the planet. The three sections, At Sea, On Land, and Skyward offer an extensive overview of the poet's life and experiences.

The images are arresting and the language lingers in the memory. This panoramic opus assures Patel a permanent place in the front rank of Asian origin poets in the West.

Hailing from East Africa rather than coming directly from India, he has a different perspective than most other subcontinentals.

Reginald Massey

Other books by Skylark Publications UK

A Certain Way by Mona Dash ISBN 9780956084040
A British debut collection by a poet who has won the Word Masala Award presented at the House of Lords

Word Masala Award Winners 2015 ISBN 9780956084033
An anthology featuring poems by Word Masala Award winners

Please visit:
http://www.skylarkpublications.co.uk/bookshop.html